Polish Cookbook

Traditional Polish Recipes
Made Easy

Table of Contents

Introduction

I want to thank you for purchasing this book, *'Polish Cookbook: Traditional Polish Recipes Made Easy.'*

Poland, much like France, is a country where people truly understand and appreciate food. Good food is part and parcel of the tradition of the land. Polish cuisine has evolved a lot over the centuries. Traditional Polish cuisine is a rich combination of aristocratic and peasant fare. It is comforting and rich at the same time.

Somewhere around A.D. 900, the Roman Catholic ritual of feasting and fasting was introduced to the land of Poland. These rituals have had a significant influence on Polish food and traditions. Polish cuisine isn't just about meat-oriented recipes but includes a variety of meatless and vegetarian dishes.

Germany and Russia are the neighboring countries to Poland. All through history, there were various instances where Poland was forced to create and form different political alliances. These alliances have a major influence on the cuisine and culture of Poland. For instance, in the sixteenth century, King Zygmunt of Poland married Bona Sforza, an Italian Princess. The Italian princess introduced Italian food and customs to Poland, including salad. In fact, in Poland, salad is known as Wloszcyna and it literally translates to "Italian things." The history of Poland is peppered with different instances like this one. Therefore, it is no wonder that Polish food exhibits the traits of other cuisines.

If you want to learn to cook traditional Polish cuisine, then there is one thing that you must stop worrying about. You need to stop counting calories and lose yourself in an intoxicating world of flavors, textures and hearty meals. A typical Polish meal is often hearty and contains a lot of meat. It isn't merely about sampling the dishes; it is about enjoying the food you cook. The most popular Polish dishes include pierogi, golabki, bigos and kotlet. Well, in this book, you will find the recipes to these famous dishes and many other authentic Polish recipes.

If you want to learn to cook traditional Polish food, then you need to be familiar with the typical ingredients that Polish cuisine features. The common ingredients include sauerkraut, beetroot, kohlrabi, mushrooms, different sausages and gherkins! The main spices that feature in Polish cuisine include dill, parsley, pepper, marjoram and caraway seeds. If you really want to indulge in a festive Polish meal, then you must not forget to serve some chilled vodka to go along with the food! Polish cuisine is all about celebrating the ingredients as well as life!

All the recipes curated in this book are not only easy to understand but are quite easy to cook as well. Be patient and carefully go through the recipes. It is quite easy to cook Polish food, if you follow the recipes given in this book. Once you get a hang of the traditional flavors and ingredients, you can experiment in the kitchen to your heart's content.

So, if you are ready to learn more about traditional Polish cuisine, then let us start without further ado.

Chapter One: Polish Breakfast Recipes

Traditional Polish Breakfast

Serves: 2

Ingredients:

- 2 Polish sausages
- 6 ounces shredded potatoes
- 2 teaspoons oil
- 2 apples, sliced
- 4 tablespoons butter
- 4 eggs
- Salt to taste
- Pepper to taste

Method:

1. Place a nonstick pan over medium high heat. Add sausages and lower the heat.
2. Cook until brown all over. Stir occasionally. Remove sausages and set aside on a plate.
3. Add half the butter. When butter melts, add half the potatoes and spread it like a pancake. Do not stir. Cook until the underside is golden brown. Flip sides and cook the other side until golden brown. Remove the potato cake and place on a plate lined with paper towels.
4. Repeat the above step and make the other potato cake.
5. Place the pan over medium heat. Add oil and let the pan heat.

6. Add eggs into a bowl and whisk well. Add salt and pepper and stir.
7. Add eggs into the pan and scramble the eggs. Cook until the eggs are cooked as per your liking.
8. To serve: Take 2 serving plates. Place a potato cake on each plate. Divide the scrambled eggs among the plates. Place a sausage in each plate. Place apple slices and serve.

Placki Ziemniaczane (Polish Potato Pancakes)

Serves: 3-4

Ingredients:

- 3 potatoes, grated
- 1 small onion, grated
- 2 tablespoons all-purpose flour
- Salt to taste
- Pepper to taste
- ½ cup sour cream + extra to serve
- 1 egg
- Vegetable oil, to fry, as required
- Sugar to sprinkle (optional)

Method:

1. Add all the ingredients into a bowl and mix well.
2. Place a small deep pan over medium heat. Pour enough oil such that it is about ¼ inch high from the bottom of the pan. Let the oil heat well, but it should not be smoking.
3. Drop about a tablespoon of the potato mixture into the hot oil. Drop 3-4 more similar pancakes into the hot oil. Fry until golden brown. Flip sides and cook until golden brown.
4. Remove with a slotted spoon and place on a plate lined with paper towels.
5. Repeat step 3-4 and make the remaining pancakes.
6. Serve warm with sour cream or sugar sprinkled on it.

Kasza Manna Semolina Porridge with Blackberry Syrup

Serves: 4

Ingredients:

- 14 ounces semolina
- A pinch salt
- 2 teaspoons sugar
- 27 ounces milk
- 10 1/2 ounces blackberries
- 6 tablespoons honey

Method:

1. Add semolina into a bowl. Add a little cold water and stir until smooth and free from lumps.
2. Add milk into a saucepan. Add salt and stir. Place the saucepan over medium heat and let the milk heat.
3. Place another pan over low heat. Add blackberries and sugar and stir. Cover and cook until the juices are released. Stir occasionally.
4. When the milk is well heated but not boiling, add semolina paste stirring constantly using a wooden spoon.
5. Lower the heat to low heat. Let it simmer for a few minutes. Stir frequently.
6. Turn off the heat. Add honey and stir.
7. Ladle into bowls. Spoon the blueberry syrup on top and serve.

Polish Sausage and Pancake Casserole

Serves: 8

Ingredients:

- 8 eggs
- 2 cups all-purpose flour
- 7 tablespoons butter
- ½ pound gouda cheese, grated
- 3 1/3 pounds spinach
- 2/3 pound cherry tomatoes, halved
- 5 cups whole milk or milk of your choice
- 4 teaspoons canola oil
- 4 cups vegetable stock
- 2 onions, finely chopped
- ¼ teaspoon grated nutmeg or to taste
- 16 Polish sausages (3 ounces each), halved lengthwise
- Salt to taste
- Pepper to taste

Method:

1. Add 2 eggs, 1-cup milk and ¼ teaspoon salt into a bowl and whisk well. Add 1 and ½ cups flour and whisk until well combined. Let it sit for 15 minutes.
2. Meanwhile make the sauce as follows: Place a saucepan over medium heat. Add butter. When butter melts, add ½ cup flour and sauté for 3-4 minutes. Stirring constantly, pour in the milk and stock. Stir until it begins to boil.
3. Stir in the cheese and let it boil for 4-5 minutes. Add salt and pepper and stir. Turn off the heat. Let it cool for a while.

4. Add remaining eggs into the sauce, one at a time and beat well each time.
5. Place a large nonstick pan over medium heat. Add 1-teaspoon oil. When the oil is heated, pour about ½ cup batter on the pan. Swirl the pan slightly so that the batter spreads.
6. Cook until the underside is golden brown. Flip sides and cook the other side.
7. Repeat steps 5-6 and make remaining pancakes.
8. Place a large pan over medium heat. Add remaining oil. When the oil is heated, add onions and sauté until translucent. Stir in the spinach, nutmeg, salt and pepper. Cook for a few minutes until spinach wilts. Turn off the heat.
9. Take a large baking dish. Place layers starting with pancake followed by some spinach mixture. Next layer with some of the sausages followed by some tomatoes. Spread a layer of the sauce.
10. Repeat the previous step and make 1-2 more set of layers.
11. Bake in a preheated oven at 350° F for about 40 minutes. If you find that the top is browning too quickly, cover the dish with foil.
12. Remove from the oven and let it sit for 10 minutes before serving.

Spiced Pumpkin Placki

Serves: 4-5 (3-4 per serving)

Ingredients:

- 14 1/2 ounces pumpkin, peeled, deseeded, finely grated
- 2 teaspoons cinnamon powder
- 3 1/2 ounces plain flour
- 1 teaspoon nutmeg powder
- Toasted almonds to serve, as required
- Honey to drizzle, as required
- Rapeseed oil, to fry, as required

Method:

1. Add pumpkin, flour, sour cream, cinnamon powder and nutmeg powder into a bowl and mix until well combined.
2. Place a nonstick pan over medium heat. Add 1-2 teaspoons oil. When the oil is heated, pour about a tablespoon of the batter. Spread it slightly. Make 3-4 more simultaneously or as many that can fit in your pan.
3. Cook for 3-4 minutes. Flip sides and cook the other side for 2-3 minutes.
4. Garnish with almonds. Drizzle honey over it and serve with sour cream.

Polish Sausage with Bacon and Broccoli

Serves: 8

Ingredients:

- 6 slices bacon, cut into thin slices, cut into bite size pieces
- 4 Polish sausage links, cut into bite size pieces
- 2 medium broccoli, cut into bite size florets
- 2 squares Land O Lakes Sauté Express Garlic and Herb

Method:

1. Place a nonstick pan over medium heat. Add bacon and cook until done. Remove bacon with a slotted spoon and place on a plate lined with paper towels.
2. Add garlic and herb squares and stir until it melts.
3. Add broccoli and sauté until broccoli turns bright green. Stir constantly.
4. Add sausages and heat for a couple of minutes.
5. Serve.

Polish Breakfast Skillet

Serves: 3

Ingredients:

- 6 eggs, beaten
- ½ package pre-sliced and peeled potatoes (about 1 ½ cups)
- Salt to taste
- 7 ounces Polska kielbasa, cut into 1 inch slices
- 1 small onion, chopped
- Pepper to taste
- 2 tablespoons oil
- 1 tablespoon oil or butter

Method:

1. Place a skillet over medium high heat. Add oil. When the oil is heated, add potato slices and onion and cook as per your liking. Remove with a slotted spoon and place on a plate lined with paper towels.
2. Add kielbasa and cook until done. Remove with a slotted spoon and place along with the potatoes.
3. Discard the fat in the pan. Add butter into the pan. When butter melts, add eggs, salt and pepper and stir. Cook until done. Transfer into a bowl.
4. Transfer the potatoes, onion and kielbasa into the bowl and toss well.
5. Serve.

Lane Kluski W Mleczku

Serves: 2-3

Ingredients:

- 2 eggs
- ½ teaspoon vanilla extract
- 27 ounces milk
- 4 tablespoons sugar or to taste
- 4 tablespoons all-purpose flour

Method:

1. Add eggs into a bowl along with salt. Whisk well.
2. Whisk in the flour, a tablespoon at a time and whisk well each time. The mixture should be free from lumps. Add vanilla and stir.
3. Place a heavy bottom saucepan over medium heat. Let the mixture heat. Stir until sugar is dissolved completely.
4. Pour the egg mixture in a thin drizzle. Cook for a minute. Turn off the heat.
5. Ladle into bowls and serve.

Polish Breakfast Sandwich # 1

Serves: 2

Ingredients:

- 2 onion rolls, split
- 6 kielbasa or 6 slices Polish sausage, thin slices, 3 inches long
- 2 slices Monterey Jack pepper cheese or sharp cheddar cheese
- 2 teaspoon butter
- 2 tablespoons mayonnaise
- 2 eggs
- Pepper to taste

Method:

1. Place a nonstick pan over medium heat.
2. Add 1-teaspoon butter. Crack an egg into the pan. Break the yolk. Sprinkle pepper.
3. Place half the sausage slices beside the egg. Cook until done. Remove carefully with a slotted spoon and place on a plate.
4. Spread mayonnaise on the cut part of the roll.
5. Place egg, cheese and sausage on the bottom half of the roll. Cover with the top half of the roll and serve.
6. Repeat steps 2-5 to make the other sandwich.

Polish Breakfast Sandwich # 2

Serves: 2

Ingredients:

- 4 slices rye bread
- 4 tomatoes, chopped
- 4 hardboiled eggs, peeled, sliced
- 3-4 tablespoons sour cream
- 2-3 tablespoons mayonnaise
- Few slices cucumber
- 4 slices turkey
- 2 scallions, chopped
- Lettuce leaves as required
- Salt to taste
- Pepper to taste

Method:

1. Spread mayonnaise on one side of the bread.
2. Take 2 slices of bread. Layer with lettuce followed by turkey slices, cucumber slices and egg slices. Sprinkle salt and pepper. Cover with the remaining 2 slices of bread.
3. Add tomatoes into a bowl. Add scallions and toss. Sprinkle salt and pepper and toss.
4. Serve sandwiches with tomato salad.

Millet Porridge

Serves: 3-4

Ingredients:

- 4-5 cups hazelnut milk or any other milk of your choice
- 1 cup dates, pitted, chopped
- ¼ teaspoon ground ginger
- 1 cup millet, rinsed, drained
- ½ teaspoon ground cinnamon
- A pinch salt

For topping:

- Fruits of your choice, chopped
- A handful toasted almond flakes or any other nuts of your choice

Method:

1. Pour milk into a saucepan. Place the saucepan over medium heat. When the milk begins to boil, stir in the millet, cinnamon and dates.
2. Lower the heat. Let it boil for a few minutes.
3. Add ginger and let it simmer for a few minutes. Add salt and continue simmering until the consistency you desire is achieved.
4. Ladle into bowls. Top with nuts and fruits and serve.

Chapter Two: Polish Appetizers / Snacks

Polish Style Nachos

Serves: 3

Ingredients:

- ½ pound kielbasa sausage
- 1 small onion, thinly sliced
- 3 tablespoons beer
- ½ tablespoon whole grain mustard
- Freshly cracked pepper to taste
- 2 whole dill pickle spears, chopped
- 1 teaspoon olive oil
- ½ can (from a 14.5 ounces can) sauerkraut
- ½ tablespoon Dijon mustard
- A pinch salt
- ¾ cup extra sharp cheddar cheese, shredded
- 7 ounces tortilla chips

Method:

1. Place a pot, half filled with water over medium heat. When it begins to boil, lower the heat and add kielbasa. Cook for 20-30 minutes or until done.
2. Drain and place kielbasa on your cutting board. When it is cool enough to handle, chop pinto smaller pieces.
3. Place the pan back over heat. Add oil. When the oil is heated, add onions and sauté until translucent. Add sauerkraut along with its juices. Sauté until sauerkraut is light brown.

4. Stir in the beer, salt, pepper, whole grain mustard and Dijon mustard.
5. Add the sausage back into the pan. Mix well. Simmer for a few minutes. Stir occasionally.
6. Add cheese and stir. When cheese melts, remove from heat.
7. Place tortilla chips on a large serving platter. Spread the sausage mixture over the chips.
8. Sprinkle dill pickle on top and serve.

Kielbasa Appetizers

Serves: 4-6

Ingredients:

- 1 pound kielbasa sausage, cut into ½ inch pieces
- 8 3/4 ounces beer
- 2 ounces brown sugar
- 9 ounces barbecue sauce
- 1 ounce Dijon mustard

Method:

1. Add beer, brown sugar, barbecue sauce and Dijon mustard into a skillet.
2. Place the skillet over medium heat. When it begins to boil, lower the heat. Add kielbasa. Mix well. Let it simmer until sausage is brown and a glaze is visible.

Śliwki w Boczku (Polish Prunes Wrapped in Bacon)

Serves: 8

Ingredients:

- 4 slices bacon, halved
- 8 prunes, pitted
- Boiling water, as required

Method:

1. Add prunes into a bowl. Pour enough boiling water so that the prunes are covered with water.
2. Drain after 15 minutes. Place prunes on layers of paper towels for a few minutes to dry.
3. Take 1 strip of bacon and wrap it around the prune. Place on a baking sheet lined with parchment paper.
4. Repeat the previous step with the remaining bacon strips and prunes.
5. Bake in a preheated oven at 350° F for about 5 minutes.
6. Turn the prunes around and bake for another 10 minutes or until crisp.
7. Remove the prunes and place on a plate lined with paper towels.
8. Insert toothpicks and serve warm.

Jajka Faszerowany (Stuffed Eggs)

Serves: 6 (half egg per serving)

Ingredients:

- 3 large eggs, hardboiled, peeled, halved lengthwise
- 2 tablespoons Polish honey cheese or any other cheese of your choice
- 1 teaspoon prepared mustard
- 1 teaspoon fresh dill or chives, finely chopped
- 1 ounce butter, melted
- 4 ounces ham, cooked, ground
- 2 tablespoons sour cream
- Salt to taste
- Pepper to taste
- ½ cup dry, fine breadcrumbs

Method:

1. Carefully remove the yolks from the egg halves and add into a bowl.
2. Add cheese, mustard, chives, ham, sour cream, salt and pepper and mix until well combined.
3. Fill this mixture into the cavities of the yolks. Place the egg halves in a baking dish. Sprinkle breadcrumbs on top. Drizzle butter over it.
4. Broil in a preheated oven until the top is golden brown. Serve warm.

Smalec (Pork Lard Spread)

Serves: 4

Ingredients:

- 18 ounces white pork fat or leaf lard, diced, ground
- 2 cloves garlic, minced
- 1 large tart apple, peeled, cored, finely chopped
- Salt to taste
- Pepper to taste
- 1 large onion, finely chopped
- ¼ cup slonina (fatty bacon), chopped
- ½ teaspoon marjoram (optional)

To serve:

- Rye bread slices
- Onion slices
- Pickles

Method:

1. Add ground pork fat into a skillet. Place the skillet over medium heat. Heat until the fat is translucent.
2. Stir in the garlic, onion and bacon. Cook until bacon is golden brown and the fat in the bacon is released.
3. Add apples, pepper, marjoram and salt. Mix well. Turn off the heat.
4. Let it cool completely. Spread over rye bread. Place onion slices on the bread. Serve with pickles.

Chapter Three: Polish Lunch Recipes

Cauliflower Bacon Salad

Serves: 6

Ingredients:

- 2 medium heads cauliflower, cut into florets
- 2 pounds bacon, cooked, crumbled
- ½ cup parmesan cheese, grated
- 1 large head iceberg lettuce, shredded
- Sugar to taste
- 2 cups mayonnaise

Method:

1. Add sugar, cheese and mayonnaise into a bowl.
2. Place cauliflower in a large serving bowl. Layer with lettuce leaves followed by the mayonnaise mixture and finally bacon.
3. Cover and refrigerate until use.
4. Fold gently and serve.

Polish Zucchini Salad

Serves: 2

Ingredients:

- 1 zucchini, thinly sliced
- 2 tablespoons plain yogurt
- 1 small clove garlic, minced
- 1 tablespoon fresh dill, chopped
- Salt to taste

Method:

1. Add yogurt, garlic, dill and salt into a bowl and stir until well combined.
2. Add zucchini and fold gently.

Chlodnik - Cold Polish Beet Soup

Serves: 8

Ingredients:

- 6 beets along with its greens, chop the beets as well and slice the leaves
- 2 cups chicken stock
- 2 eggs, hardboiled, peeled, chopped
- 6 small green onions, thinly sliced
- 1 cup sour cream
- Pepper to taste
- Water, as required
- 2 small cucumbers, peeled, grated
- 2/3 cup fresh dill, chopped
- 4 cups buttermilk
- 2 tablespoons lemon juice

Method:

1. Place beets in a pot. Cover with water. Place the pot over medium heat. Cook until the beets are cooked.
2. Turn off the heat and add stock. Mix well. Let it cool completely.
3. Add cucumbers, dill, eggs and green onions into a bowl and stir. Transfer into the bowl of beets.
4. Add buttermilk and sour cream into another bowl and whisk. Transfer into the bowl of beets.
5. Mix well. Cover and chill for a few hours.
6. Serve.

Bean and Sausage Stew

Serves: 8

Ingredients:

- 2 cups dry cannellini beans, rinsed, soaked in water overnight
- 20 slices bacon, cubed
- 4 onions, chopped
- 8 allspice berries
- 1 teaspoon dried marjoram or to taste
- Salt to taste
- Pepper to taste
- 2 tablespoons all-purpose flour
- 2 tablespoons vegetable oil
- 32 ounces kielbasa sausage, cubed
- 4 bay leaves
- 2 cans (14.5 ounces each) chopped tomatoes
- 2 cloves garlic, peeled, minced
- 2 tablespoons butter
- 2 teaspoons paprika (optional)

Method:

1. Drain the cannellini beans and place in a pot. Pour enough water to cover the beans.
2. Place the pot over high heat. When the water begins to boil, lower the heat and cover with a lid. Cook until soft. Alternately, you can cook in an instant pot or pressure cooker. It will be much quicker.
3. Place a skillet over medium high heat. Add oil. When the oil is heated, add bacon and sausage and sauté until brown. Remove with a slotted spoon and place in a bowl.

4. Add onions into the skillet and sauté until brown. Transfer into the pot of cooked beans. Add bay leaves, allspice and the cooked meat. When it begins to boil, lower the heat and simmer for a few minutes.

5. Add marjoram, tomatoes, salt, pepper and garlic and stir. Simmer for 15-20 minutes. If the stew is very dry, add some water.

6. Place a small saucepan over low heat. Add butter. When butter melts, add flour and sauté for about a minute. Turn off the heat and transfer into the pot. Mix well

7. Add paprika and simmer until the stew is thickened as per your liking.

8. Stir the meat mixture, allspice and bay leaves in the beans allow it to simmer. Add garlic, marjoram, tomatoes, salt, and pepper and let it simmer for another 10 to 15 minutes. Add water if there is not enough liquid in the pot.

9. Melt butter in a small saucepan over low heat, add flour, and stir into a paste. Take it off the heat and add it to the stew then add paprika powder. Simmer for about 15 minutes or until the stew thickens.

Polish Sandwich

Serves: 4

Ingredients:

- 10-11 ounces shaved pork smoked meat
- 1 cup sour cream
- 2 small cloves garlic, pressed
- Pickled pepper to taste
- 8 slices salami
- 6 tablespoons old fashioned mustard
- 4 slices dill pickle
- 4 poppy seed bagels, split, toasted
- A few bell pepper slices

Method:

1. Add mustard, sour cream, salt, pepper and garlic into a bowl. Mix until well combined.
2. Place pork meat and salami on the bottom halves of the bagels.
3. Spread some of the sour cream mixture. Top with dill pickle and pepper slices. Cover with the top half of the bagels.
4. Serve right away with the remaining sour cream mixture.

Polish Sausage Sandwich

Serves: 2

Ingredients:

- ½ pound Polish sausage (kielbasa), cut into ¼ inch rounds
- 2 submarine rolls, split
- A little horseradish (optional)
- 8 ounces sauerkraut, drained
- Mustard of your choice, as required
- Cheese slices, as required (optional)

Method:

1. Place sausage slices on the bottom halves of the submarine rolls.
2. Spread some sauerkraut over it. Place cheese slices if using.
3. Spread horseradish if using on the cut part of the top of the rolls.
4. Close the sandwich with the top part of the roll with the cut side facing down.
5. Place the bun on a large sheet of foil and wrap it.
6. Bake in a preheated oven at 350° F for about 15 minutes or until heated thoroughly and the bun is slightly toasted.

Zapiekanka

Serves: 2

Ingredients:

- ½ loaf French bread
- 1 cup sautéed mushrooms
- Mayonnaise, as required
- 1-2 tablespoons ketchup
- ½ cup thinly sliced ham or lunch meat of your choice or more if required
- Few tomato slices
- Few cucumber slices
- Any other cooked or grilled vegetables of your choice (optional)
- ½ cup melting cheese of your choice, grated
- 1 tablespoon chopped chives

Method:

1. Cut the bread into 2 halves vertically. Cut each piece into 2 horizontally.
2. Place a layer of meat on each of the cut slices of bread. Layer with tomato, cucumber, mushrooms and any other vegetables if using. Sprinkle cheese on top.
3. Bake in a preheated oven at 350° F for about 8 -10 minutes or the bread is crisp and the cheese melts.
4. Dot with ketchup and serve immediately.

Chapter Four: Polish Dinner Recipes

Soups and Stews:

Rosol (Polish Chicken Noodle Soup)

Serves: 3-4

Ingredients:

- 1 pound chicken thighs
- 1 small parsnip, halved
- 1 small onion, halved
- A handful fresh parsley, chopped
- Pepper to taste
- Salt to taste
- Noodles of your choice, cooked according the instructions on the package, to serve

Method:

1. Place a pot half filled with water over medium heat. Add chicken.
2. Meanwhile, place a pan over medium heat. Place onion with cut side down. Cook until slightly charred.
3. When it begins to boil, lower the heat. Add parsnip, carrot and onion and cover with a lid. Simmer for about 1 hour. Discard the vegetables.
4. Ladle broth and chicken into bowls. Add noodles into the bowls. Garnish with parsley and serve.

Najlepsza Zupa Ogorkowa (Polish Pickled Cucumber Soup)

Serves: 8

Ingredients:

- 2 jars (32 ounces each) pickled cucumbers, drained, grated
- 1 bunch celery, sliced
- 1-2 ham bones (optional)
- 2 leeks, sliced
- 6 whole allspice berries
- 6 potatoes, diced
- 2 tablespoons fresh marjoram, chopped
- ¼ cup heavy whipping cream
- 4 carrots, sliced
- 2 onions, chopped
- 2 bunches parsley, chopped
- Water, as required
- 8 cloves garlic, crushed
- Salt to taste
- Pepper to taste
- 2 tablespoons all-purpose flour

Method:

1. Add grated pickle into a saucepan. Pour about ½ cup water. Place the saucepan over medium heat. Cook until soft.
2. Add celery, ham bone, parsley, carrots, onions, allspice and leeks into a soup pot. Pour enough water to cover.

3. When it begins to boil, lower the heat and simmer for about an hour.
4. Add garlic and potatoes and cook until potatoes are tender. Discard the ham bone.
5. Add grated pickle along with the cooked water. Add salt, pepper and marjoram.
6. Whisk together cream and flour in a bowl until free from lumps. Pour into the soup.
7. Stir constantly for a few minutes until thick.
8. Ladle into soup bowls and serve.

Polish Beet Soup

Serves: 3

Ingredients:

- 3 beets along with its greens, chop the beets as well and slice the leaves and stems
- 1 leek, white and light green parts only, chopped
- ½ cup carrots, cubed
- 3 cups chicken broth
- ¼ pound celery root, peeled, cut into ½ inch cubes
- 3 eggs, hardboiled, peeled, quartered lengthwise
- 1 ½ cups cubed potatoes
- 1 small parsnip, peeled, cut into ½ inch cubes
- 3 tablespoons sour cream
- Pepper to taste
- ½ tablespoon white sugar
- Salt to taste
- ½ tablespoon lemon juice or to taste
- 2 tablespoons all-purpose flour

Method:

1. Add beets, celery root, parsnip, carrot, leek and broth into a soup pot.
2. Place the soup pot over medium heat. When it begins to boil, lower the heat and add potatoes. Cook until soft.
3. Add beet greens and stems and cook until the stems are tender. Add lemon juice, sugar, pepper and salt and stir.
4. Whisk together flour and sour cream into a bowl and pour into the simmering soup. Stir constantly until thick.

31

5. Stir in the dill. Turn off the heat.
6. Serve in bowls topped with 1 egg in each bowl.

Polish Borscht

Serves: 8

Ingredients:

- 3 pounds pork spareribs
- 2 bay leaves
- 4 tablespoons white vinegar
- 4 cups sour cream
- 6 tablespoons flour
- 2 large onions, chopped
- 6 whole peppercorns
- 10 medium beets
- 4 cups milk
- Salt to taste
- Pepper to taste

Method:

1. Place a large soup pot over medium heat. Add spare ribs, bay leaves, vinegar, onion and peppercorns into the pot. Pour enough water to cover.
2. Place the pot over medium heat. When it begins to boil, lower the heat and cook until meat is tender.
3. Meanwhile, add beets in another pot. Cover with water. Place the pot over medium heat. Cook until the beets are cooked through.
4. Drain the beets and submerge in cold water. When the beets are cooled, peel the beets. Grate the beets and set aside.
5. When the meat is cooked, remove the meat with a slotted spoon and place on your cutting board. When cool enough to handle, remove meat from the bones

and cut into bite size pieces. Add it back into the simmering soup. Add beets, salt and pepper.

6. Whisk together milk, sour cream and flour in a bowl and pour into the soup. Stir constantly until the soup thickens. Do not boil the soup.

7. Serving options: Rye bread or boiled potatoes or anything of your choice.

Bigos (Polish Hunter's Stew)

Serves: 3-4

Ingredients:

- 1 ½ pounds sauerkraut, rinsed, drained, chopped
- 4 ½ cups boiling water, divided
- 7-8 prunes, pitted
- 2 bay leaves
- 1 tablespoon vegetable oil
- ½ Polish sausage
- 4 ounces pork shoulder, cubed
- 4 ounces beef stew meat, cubed
- ¼ cup chopped bacon strips
- 2 teaspoons dried marjoram
- 1/3 cup red wine
- ½ tablespoon caraway seeds
- 1 ½ tablespoons tomato paste (optional)
- 1 onion, chopped
- ½ cup dried mushrooms
- 2-3 whole allspice berries
- Salt to taste
- Pepper to taste

Method:

1. Add sauerkraut into a pan. Pour 2 cups boiling water over it. Stir in the prunes, bay leaves and allspice.
2. Place the pan over medium heat. When the mixture begins to boil, lower the heat and cover with a lid. Simmer for 30-40 minutes. Turn off heat when soft.
3. Place dried mushrooms in a bowl. Pour ½ cup boiling water over it. Let it soak for 30 minutes. Place a

35

strainer over a bowl and strain the mushrooms. Retain the soaked liquid.

4. When cool enough to handle, chop the mushroom into smaller pieces.
5. Place a pan over medium-high heat. Add oil. When the oil is heated, add onion and sausage and cook until the sausage is brown. Stir frequently.
6. Pour remaining water into a pan. Place the pan over medium heat.
7. When the water begins to boil, add all the 3 types of meat. Cook until tender. Drain and add into the cooked sauerkraut. Also add the sausage mixture and mushrooms and stir. Do not cover.
8. Lower the heat and simmer for 15 minutes.
9. Add wine and simmer for 10-12 minutes. Add marjoram, caraway seeds, pepper, salt and tomato paste if using. Add the retained water of the mushrooms. Mix well.
10. Continue simmering for 5-6 minutes.
11. Ladle into bowls and serve.

Polish Goulash (Beef Stew)

Serves: 3

Ingredients:

- 1 ¼ pound tender cut of beef preferably sirloin steak, chopped into chunks
- 1 tablespoon extra-virgin olive oil
- 1 package mushrooms, chopped into chunks
- ½ cup red bell pepper, chopped into squares
- 3 medium onions, chopped into chunks
- 3-4 cloves garlic, minced
- 1 small bay leaf
- ½ tablespoon sugar
- 1 tablespoon caraway seeds
- 1 ½ tablespoons fresh marjoram
- Salt to taste
- 2 tablespoons tomato paste or to taste
- ½ teaspoon allspice powder
- ½ teaspoon dried thyme
- ½ teaspoon cumin powder
- 1 tablespoon sweet paprika
- 1 teaspoon spicy paprika
- 2 cups chicken stock
- Freshly ground pepper to taste

To serve:

- Sour cream
- Egg noodles (optional)
- Potato cheese pierogi (optional)

Method:

1. Add all the ingredients into a Dutch oven or a slow cooker. Mix well.

2. Cover and cook over low heat until meat is tender.
3. Serve over egg noodles or potato cheese pierogi. Drizzle sour cream on top and serve.

Okragly Chleb Kartoflany (Polish Potato Bread)

Makes: 2 loaves

Ingredients:

- 1 cup freshly mashed potatoes
- 1 cup milk
- 4 tablespoons butter, softened
- 2 large eggs, beaten
- ½ cup warm water
- 6 tablespoons sugar
- 6 cups all-purpose flour, divided
- 4 ½ teaspoons yeast (active dry or rapid-rise or instant yeast)
- 2 teaspoons salt

Method:

1. Pour milk into a saucepan. Place the saucepan over medium heat. Heat the milk up to 180 °F. Turn off the heat.
2. Pour the milk into a large mixing bowl. Stir in the potatoes, butter and sugar and mix well using your hands. Let it cool for a while.
3. Add half the flour and egg and continue mixing by hand until well incorporated. Set aside for a while.
4. Add warm water and yeast into a bowl. When the yeast dissolves completely, pour into the potato mixture. Add salt and mix until well combined.
5. Grease a plastic wrap and cover the bowl. Place the bowl in a warm place for 1-½ hours.
6. Set the dough hook attachment of the stand mixer. Add rest of the flour and knead using the mixer for 7 minutes.

7. Take a bowl and grease with a little oil. Transfer the dough into this bowl. Cover the bowl with a greased plastic wrap and set aside in a warm place until the dough doubles in size.

8. Divide the dough into 2 equal portions. Punch the dough with your fist and shape into round loaves. Place on 2 baking pans with parchment paper. Cover the pans with greased plastic wrap. Place in a warm place until it doubles in size.

9. Uncover and make "X' (about 2 cm deep) using a knife on the top of the loaves.

10. Bake in a preheated oven at 350° F for about 30-45 minutes or until done. Bake in batches if required.

11. Remove the baking pan from the oven and cool for a few minutes. Remove the bread from the baking pan and place on a wire rack. When it cools completely, slice.

12. Spread butter lightly on the bread slices and serve.

Polish Sourdough Rye Bread

Serves: 18

Ingredients:

- 1 package (0.25 ounce) active dry yeast
- 1 cup water
- ½ cup buttermilk, at room temperature
- ½ tablespoon salt
- ½ teaspoon white sugar
- 2 cups rye flour
- 4 cups bread flour
- ½ teaspoon baking powder
- ½ tablespoon caraway seeds

Method:

1. Add 1-cup water and ½ packet yeast into a bowl. In a few minutes it will be frothy.
2. Add rye flour and mix until well combined and free from lumps. Cover and set aside for 7-8 hours.
3. When 7-8 hours are completed, add ½ package yeast into a large bowl along with buttermilk. Let the yeast dissolve completely.
4. Stir in the rye flour mixture along with salt, baking soda and 2 cups bread flour. Mix until well incorporated.
5. Add ½ cup of the remaining bread flour. Mix well. Continue adding ½ cup flour and mixing well each time until all the flour is added.
6. Mix into smooth dough.
7. Dust your countertop lightly with a little flour. Knead the dough for 8-9 minutes until smooth.

8. Scatter caraway seeds and knead for a couple of minutes. Transfer into a clean greased bowl. Turn the dough around in the bowl so that the dough is lightly coated with oil.

9. Cover the bowl with a moist cloth and place the bowl in a warm place until the dough doubles in size. Punch lightly the dough.

10. Transfer the dough into a large greased bread pan. Cover the pan and set aside for a while until it doubles in size.

11. Bake in a preheated oven at 350° F for about 30-45 minutes or until done. When you tap the bread on the bottom, if you hear a hollow sound, the bread is ready.

12. Cool completely. Slice and serve.

Piernik (Honey Bread)

Serves: 16

Ingredients:

- ½ cup sugar
- ¼ teaspoon ground cloves
- 2 eggs
- ¼ cup vegetable oil
- ½ cup honey
- ¼ cup raisins (optional)
- ½ teaspoon ground cinnamon
- ¼ teaspoon ground allspice
- ¼ cup milk
- ½ teaspoon baking soda
- 2 cups all-purpose flour
- ¼ cup walnuts (optional)

Method:

1. Add sugar, eggs and all the spices into a large bowl and stir.
2. Add milk and oil and whisk until well combined. Add baking soda and mix well.
3. Add honey into a small pot and place the pot over medium heat. Turn off the heat when it begins to boil. Transfer into the bowl of egg mixture and mix well.
4. Add flour and mix well. Add raisins and walnuts if using and stir using a wooden spoon for about 8-10 minutes.
5. Let the dough rest for an hour.
6. Grease 2 small loaf pans with a little oil. Pour batter equally into the pans (it should cover about 2 inches from the bottom of the pan).

7. Bake in a preheated oven at 325° F for about 60-75 minutes or until done. Also the top will be brown and cracked as well.

8. Remove the baking pans from the oven and cool for a few minutes. Remove the bread from the baking pans and place on a wire rack. When it cools completely, slice and serve.

Side Dishes:

Mizeria (Cucumber Salad)

Serves: 6

Ingredients:

- ½ pound small cucumbers, peeled, thinly sliced
- ½ bunch dill, chopped
- Lemon juice to taste
- Pepper to taste
- Salt to taste
- 3 teaspoons sour cream
- A pinch white sugar

Method:

1. Place cucumber slices in a colander. Sprinkle salt over it. Let it drain for 5 minutes.
2. Squeeze the cucumbers of excess moisture. Place cucumbers in a bowl. Add rest of the ingredients and toss well.
3. Chill for 30 minutes and serve.

Authentic Polish Vegetable Salad

Serves: 3-4

Ingredients:

- 4 small potatoes, cooked, cut into small cubes
- ½ can carrots, drained, cut into small pieces
- ½ can peas, drained
- ½ stalk celery, chopped
- 1-2 pickles, chopped
- 1 small apple, cored, chopped
- 1 teaspoon lemon juice
- Salt to taste
- Pepper to taste
- ¼ cup mayonnaise
- Paprika to taste
- ½ teaspoon mustard
- 1-2 tablespoons fresh dill, chopped

Method:

1. Gather all the ingredients and add into a bowl. Toss well.
2. Taste and adjust the seasonings and mayonnaise if required.
3. Serve.

Stewed Cabbage

Serves: 2

Ingredients:

- 1 small head cabbage, cut into squares
- 1 onion, chopped
- 1 clove garlic, chopped
- 1 small stalk celery, chopped
- 2 tablespoons butter
- Pepper to taste
- Salt to taste
- ½ can (from a 14.5 ounces can) stewed tomatoes with its liquid

Method:

1. Place a saucepan over medium heat. Add butter. When butter melts, add garlic, onion and celery and sauté until onions are translucent.
2. Add cabbage and mix well. Lower the heat and simmer for 10-12 minutes.
3. Add tomatoes, salt and pepper and stir. Cover and cook for 20-30 minutes until cabbage is cooked.
4. Stir and serve.

Pieczarki Marynowane

Serves: 2

Ingredients:

- 1 pound medium size fresh button mushrooms, cleaned

For salted water:

- 10 tablespoons water
- 2 whole allspice berries
- 1 bay leaf, crushed
- ½ cup 6% distilled vinegar
- 5 whole peppercorns
- 2 whole cloves
- 2 teaspoons salt
- 1-4 tablespoons sugar, depending on how sweet you desire

Method:

1. Place a pot half filled with water over medium heat. When the water begins to boil, add mushrooms and boil for 15 minutes.
2. Place another pot over medium heat. Add all the ingredients for salted water. When the mixture begins to boil, lower the heat and simmer for 10 minutes. Turn off the heat.
3. Drain and add mushrooms into a sterilized jar. Pour marinade over it. Fasten the lid of the jar and place in the refrigerator until use.

Potato Dumplings

Serves: 8

Ingredients:

- 4 hard rolls (a day old), torn into ½ inch pieces
- 4 teaspoons canola oil
- 2 eggs, lightly beaten
- 3-4 tablespoons all-purpose flour
- 1 cup water
- 1 cup leftover mashed potatoes
- ¼ teaspoon ground nutmeg
- ½ cup butter, cubed

Method:

1. Place torn rolls in a baking dish. Spread it in the dish. Sprinkle water over the bread. Squeeze the bread pieces until dry.
2. Place a large skillet over medium high heat. Add oil. When the oil is heated, add squeezed roll pieces and sauté for a couple of minutes until it is toasted slightly.
3. Transfer into a bowl. Add potatoes, nutmeg and eggs and mix well. Add 3 tablespoons flour and mix well. Add more flour if necessary, 1 tablespoon at a time and mix well each time.
4. Dust your hands with flour and make balls of 3 inches diameter.
5. Place a large pot half filled with water over medium high heat. When the water begins to boil, lower the heat and drop the dumplings into the simmering water. Do not cover while it is cooking.

6. Let it simmer for 8-10 minutes. When the dumplings are cooked, a toothpick when inserted in the center should come out clean. Remove with a slotted spoon and place on a plate.
7. Add butter into a small saucepan. Place the saucepan over low heat. When the butter melts, turn off the heat.
8. Serve warm dumplings with melted butter.

Befszytk Tatarski (Polish Steak Tartare)

Serves: 3

Ingredients:

For tartare:

- ½ pound good quality beef tenderloin, rinsed, finely chopped or coarsely ground
- ½ tablespoon olive oil
- ½ teaspoon parsley, minced
- ½ tablespoon Polish grainy mustard or any other spicy brown mustard
- 1 small pasteurized egg yolk
- Salt to taste
- Pepper to taste

For garnishing:

- 1 small pasteurized egg yolk
- 1 small dill pickle, finely chopped
- 1 small onion, finely chopped
- 3 teaspoons capers
- 3 slices bread, trim the sides, cut each into 2 triangles, toasted
- Anchovies, to taste, chopped

Method:

1. For steak tartare: Add beef, mustard, egg yolk, oil, salt pepper and parsley into a bowl and mix until well combined. Make it into a heap and place on a plate.
2. For garnishing: Make a depression in the center and place yolk in it. Sprinkle onion, dill pickle, capers and anchovies all around the tartare.
3. Serve right away with toasted bread triangles.

Kotlety Mielone

Serves: 6-8

Ingredients:

- 2 1/4 pounds minced meat
- 2 cups milk
- 2 eggs
- 1 cup breadcrumbs, or as required
- 2 bread rolls
- 1 large onion, chopped
- Salt to taste
- Pepper to taste
- Oil for frying, as required

Method:

1. Add milk into a bowl. Place the bread rolls in it for a few minutes.
2. Add meat into a large bowl. Squeeze the bread of excess milk and add into the bowl of meat.
3. Stir in the eggs, onion, salt and pepper and mix well.
4. Make cutlets of the mixture.
5. Place breadcrumbs in a shallow bowl. Dredge the cutlets in the breadcrumbs.
6. Place a nonstick skillet over medium heat. Add 2-3 tablespoons oil. When the oil is heated, place 2-3 cutlets on it. Cook until the underside is golden brown. Flip sides and cook the other side is golden brown.
7. Repeat the previous step and cook the remaining cutlets.
8. Serve hot.

Papryka Nadziewana

Serves: 8

Ingredients:

- 8 bell peppers of any color
- 2 pounds ground beef
- 2 cloves garlic, minced
- 2 large eggs
- 2 teaspoons salt or to taste
- 8 tomato slices
- Salt to taste
- Pepper to taste
- 2 medium onions, finely chopped
- 2 cups cooked rice or barley or buckwheat groats
- 2 teaspoons paprika
- 1 teaspoon pepper or to taste
- 4 cups tomato juice

Serving options:

- Dumplings
- Potatoes
- Noodles

Method:

1. Slice off the tops of the peppers. Set aside the tops. Discard the seeds and membranes. Sprinkle salt and pepper inside the peppers.
2. Grease a large baking dish with cooking spray.
3. Finely chop the tops of the bell peppers and place in a large bowl. Also add ground meat (brown the meat if desired), garlic, onion, eggs, salt, pepper, rice and paprika and mix well.

4. Fill this mixture into the bell peppers and place in the greased baking dish. Place a slice of tomato in each pepper. Pour tomato juice all over the peppers.
5. Cover the dish tightly with foil.
6. Bake in a preheated oven at 350° F for about 50-70 minutes. If the juice is getting dry, then pour a little water.
7. Serve with any one or more of the serving options.

Veal Paprikash

Serves: 5 (1 cup stew with ¾ cup noodles)

Ingredients:

- 2 tablespoons margarine, divided
- 2 lean veal tip round roast (2 ¼ pounds each), cut into 1 inch pieces
- 2 cups onions, sliced
- 3 cups carrots, sliced
- ½ cup all-purpose flour
- 1 teaspoon salt or to taste
- 2 ounces garlic cloves, minced
- A handful parsley, chopped
- 2 tablespoons paprika
- 1 teaspoon pepper
- 1 teaspoon salt
- 2 cups beef broth
- 2 cups chicken broth
- 1 cup dry white wine
- 1 cup low fat sour cream
- 4 bay leaves
- 10 ½ cups hot, cooked, medium egg noodles

Method:

1. Place a Dutch oven over medium high heat. Spray with cooking spray. Add 2 teaspoons margarine. When margarine melts, add veal and cook until brown all over. Remove veal and place on a plate lined with paper towels.
2. Place a pan over medium heat. Add 4 teaspoons margarine. When it melts, stir in the onion, carrot and garlic and sauté for a few minutes until tender.

3. Add flour, salt, pepper and paprika. Stir for 20-30 seconds.
4. Pour both the broths and wine. Add bay leaves and mix well. Stir constantly until the mixture thickens.
5. Add meat and stir. When it begins to boil, lower the heat and cover with a lid. Cook for about 1 ½ hours or until the meat is cooked through. Stir occasionally.
6. Remove the bay leaves and discard it.
7. Add sour cream and stir. Heat for 5-6 minutes and turn off the heat.
8. Place ¾ noodles on each plate. Ladle 1-cup veal paprikash over it. Sprinkle parsley on top and serve.

Salmon Roulade

Serves: 10-12

Ingredients:

- 2 packages (10 ounces each) fresh or frozen spinach, thawed if frozen and cook until it wilts if fresh
- 17 ounces smoked salmon slices
- 8 eggs, separated
- 2 packages (7 ounces each) full fat cream cheese
- 2 teaspoons lemon zest, grated
- Salt to taste
- Freshly ground pepper to taste
- Juice of a lemon
- A handful fresh dill, chopped

Method:

1. Whisk the whites until stiff. Add yolks and beat. Add spinach, salt and pepper and stir.
2. Transfer into a Swiss roll tin that is lined with parchment paper.
3. Bake in a preheated oven at 350° F for about 10 minutes or until it feels firm.
4. Place a large sheet of parchment paper on your countertop. Invert the cooked roulade on to the parchment paper. Let it cool. Carefully remove the parchment paper.
5. Mix together in a bowl, cream cheese, lemon zest, salt, pepper, lemon juice and dill into a bowl.
6. Spread this mixture on the roulade. Place the smoked salmon all over the roulade. Roll the roulade tightly with the help of the parchment paper.
7. Chill for 2-3 hours.

8. Slice and serve.

Polish Meat and Potatoes

Serves: 8

Ingredients:

- 8 potatoes, peeled, cut into 1 inch cubes
- 4 green bell peppers, cut into 1 inch squares
- 1 teaspoon garlic powder
- 1 teaspoon onion powder
- 1 teaspoon salt
- ½ cup oil
- ½ teaspoon pepper powder
- 2 packages (16 ounces each) kielbasa sausage, cut into 1 inch pieces

Method:

1. Place a large skillet over medium high heat. Add oil. When the oil is heated, add onions and potatoes and cook for about 15 minutes. Stir occasionally.
2. Lower the heat and add bell pepper, salt, garlic and onion powders. Mix well. Cover with a lid. Let it cook for 5-6 minutes.
3. Add sausage and stir. Cover and cook until the onions are golden brown.
4. Serve hot.

Kaszanka (Polish Black Pudding with Caramelized Onion)

Serves: 2

Ingredients:

- 2 kaszanka sausage or black pudding sausage, cut each into 4-5 rings on the diagonal
- 4 tablespoons oil
- 2 red or brown onions, thinly sliced
- Freshly ground pepper to taste

To serve:

- Rye bread slices, as required

Method:

1. Place a large pan over medium heat. Add oil. When the oil is heated, add onion and pepper powder and sauté for 2 -3 minutes. Move the onions to one side of the pan.
2. Add sausage and cook for 2 minutes. Flip sides and cook the other side of the sausage slices for 2 minutes or until brown and with a crunch.
3. Serve with rye bread slices.

Polish Perogies

Makes: 8-10

Ingredients:

- 2 ¼ cups all-purpose flour
- 1 tablespoon butter, melted
- Yolk of 1 small egg
- 1 egg
- 4 baking potatoes, peeled, cubed
- 1 tablespoon processed cheese sauce
- Salt to taste
- Pepper to taste
- 1 cup sour cream
- 1 tablespoon vegetables oil
- ½ cup cheddar cheese, shredded
- Onion salt to taste (optional)

Method:

1. Add flour and salt into a large bowl and stir.
2. Add sour cream, butter, oil egg and yolk into another bowl and whisk well. Pour into the bowl of flour and mix until smooth dough is formed.
3. Cover with a clean kitchen towel and set aside for 15-20 minutes.
4. Meanwhile, cook potatoes in a pot, covered with water. Cook until soft.
5. Drain the water and add into a bowl. Mash the potatoes while it is hot with a potato masher, along with cheese and cheese sauce.
6. Dust your countertop lightly with flour. Shape the dough into a ball and place the dough on your

countertop. Roll with a rolling pin until slightly thin but not very thin.

7. Cut into circles using a perogie cutter or a cookie cutter.

8. Place filling on one half of the circles. Do not place filling on the edges. Fold the other half over the filling. Press the edges to seal well. Place on a baking sheet.

9. Place the baking sheet in the freezer until the perogies are frozen.

10. Transfer into a freezer safe container and freeze until use.

11. To use: Boil water in a pot with a little salt added to it. Add one perogie at a time into the boiling water. When the perogies are cooked, they will float on the top of the water.

12. Remove as and when they float to the top with a slotted spoon. Place on a plate lined with paper towels.

13. Serve hot or warm.

Cheesy Kielbasa with Beans

Serves: 6

Ingredients:

- ½ pound ground chuck
- 1 medium onion, chopped
- ½ can (from a 10 ounces can) diced tomatoes with green chilies, with its liquid
- 1 can (10.75 ounces) tomato soup, undiluted
- 2 cans (16 ounces each) pinto beans, with its liquid
- ½ package (from a 16 ounce package) kielbasa sausage, thinly sliced
- 2 cans (15 ounces each) pork and beans with its liquid
- ½ can (from a 14 ½ ounces can) diced tomatoes, with its liquid
- Salt to taste
- 1 small green bell pepper, chopped
- 1 cup cheddar cheese, shredded

Method:

1. Place a Dutch oven over medium high heat. Add chuck, bell pepper and onion and sauté until it is not pink anymore. Break it simultaneously as it cooks. Remove with a slotted spoon and place on a plate lined with paper towels. Drain fat from the pot
2. Add sausage into the pot and cook until brown. Discard fat in the pot.
3. Add the beef mixture back into the pot. Add rest of the ingredients except cheese and stir.
4. Lower the heat and cover with a lid. Cook until meat is tender.

5. Alternately, you can brown the meat mixture and sausage in a skillet and transfer into a slow cooker. Cook on Low for 7-8 hours.

Polish Sloppy Joes

Serves: 10

Ingredients:

- 1 ½ pounds lean ground beef
- 15 ounces chicken broth, boiling hot
- 1 stalk celery, chopped
- Salt to taste
- Pepper to taste
- 16 ounces sauerkraut with caraway seeds
- 1 small green bell pepper, deseeded, chopped
- 1 medium onion, chopped
- Hard rolls or Semmel (Kaiser) roll, to serve

Method:

1. Place a skillet over medium-high heat. Add beef and cook until it is not brown anymore. Break it simultaneously as it cooks.
2. Add rest of the ingredients and stir. Lower the heat and simmer for an hour.
3. Add salt and pepper and serve over rolls.

Polish Style Lasagna

Serves: 4

Ingredients:

- 6 uncooked lasagna noodles, cook following the instructions on the package
- 6 tablespoons butter
- 6 ounces cream cheese
- 1 medium onion, sliced
- 1 ½ cups dry potato flakes (instant mashed potatoes), cook following the instructions on the package but do not add milk

Method:

1. Dry the lasagna sheets by patting with paper towels.
2. Place in between moist kitchen towels or spray the noodles with cooking spray.
3. Place a skillet over medium heat. Add butter. When butter melts, add onion and cook until translucent.
4. Add cream cheese into the mashed potato and mix well.
5. Grease a rectangular baking dish with a little cooking spray.
6. Lay 2 lasagna sheets in the baking dish. Layer with half the mashed potato.
7. Repeat the previous step once more.
8. Lay 2 lasagna sheets over the mashed potato. Sprinkle sautéed onion on top.
9. Bake in a preheated oven at 350° F for about 20 minutes or until the lasagna is bubbling.
10. Remove from the oven and let it sit for 5 minutes.
11. Slice and serve.

Traditional Polish Style Stuffed Cabbage Rolls

Serves: 6-7

Ingredients:

<u>For the filling:</u>

- ¼ pound ground pork
- ½ pound lean cut ground beef
- ¼ cup onion, chopped
- ½ cup cooked rice
- 1 clove garlic, minced

<u>For sauce:</u>

- 1 ½ tablespoons butter
- ¾ cup tomato juice
- ½ tablespoon cane sugar
- A pinch garlic powder
- 1 ½ tablespoons white whole wheat flour
- 1 tablespoon ketchup
- Salt to taste

<u>For cabbage:</u>

- 6-7 cabbage leaves + extra to lay in the baking dish

Method:

1. To boil the cabbage leaves: Place a pot filled with water over medium heat. Bring to a boil. Add the cabbage leaves and cook for 5-7 minutes or until soft.

69

Turn the cabbage leaves after about 4 minutes of cooking.

2. Remove the leaves with a slotted spoon or tongs and set aside on a clean kitchen towel.

3. Place a few cabbage leaves on the bottom of a square baking dish. Set aside. Remove the core with a sharp knife.

4. To make sauce: Place a small saucepan over medium-low heat. Add butter. When butter melts, add flour and stir constantly for a couple of minutes until lightly toasted.

5. Add rest of the ingredients stirring constantly. Lower the heat and cook for 15 minutes. Turn off the heat. Spread a little of the sauce over the cabbage leaves in the prepared baking dish.

6. To make filling: Add all the filling ingredients into a bowl and mix well with your hands.

7. Divide the mixture into 6-7 portions (depending on the number of cabbage leaves) and shape into a cylindrical shape (smaller than the cabbage leaf).

8. Place each meat portion in a cabbage leaf. Fold like a burrito and place in the prepared baking dish. Spread remaining sauce over it. Place some more cabbage leaves if you desire.

9. Cover the dish with foil.

10. Bake in a preheated oven at 350° F for about 30-40 minutes.

11. Remove from the oven. Let it rest for 8-10 minutes before serving.

Mashed Potatoes & Mushroom Gravy

Serves: 6-8

Ingredients:

For mashed potatoes:

- 2 ½ pounds potatoes, peeled, cut into 1 inch pieces
- 1 teaspoon salt
- Water, as required
- ¼ cup sour cream
- 2 tablespoons butter
- 1 clove garlic, minced (optional)

For mushroom gravy:

- 3 ½ cups wild mushrooms
- 1 large onion, halved, sliced
- ¼ teaspoon dried thyme
- ¼ teaspoon dried marjoram
- ½ tablespoon fresh dill, chopped
- ¼ - ½ cup sour cream
- Freshly ground pepper to taste
- Salt to taste
- 2 tablespoons butter
- ¼ cup chicken broth
- 1-2 tablespoons flour (optional)

Method:

1. Place potatoes in a large pot and cover with water. Add some salt. Place the pot over medium heat. Cook until fork tender. Drain.

2. Meanwhile, make the gravy as follows: Place a pan over medium heat. Add oil. When the oil is heated, add onion and sauté until light brown.

3. Stir in the mushrooms. Sauté for a few minutes. Add herbs, salt, pepper and broth and cook for 4-5 minutes.

4. Stir in flour and sour cream. Sprinkle flour if using. Do not add in one go - just sprinkle it. Or mix flour in a little water and add into the pan.

5. Lower the heat and simmer for 7-8 minutes or until mushroom is cooked.

6. Add dill and serve.

7. Mash the cooked potatoes with a potato masher. Add butter, salt, pepper, sour cream and garlic if using and mix well.

8. Spoon mashed potatoes on serving plates. Serve mushroom gravy over the mashed potatoes.

9. Serve hot.

Noga Jagniecia (Roast Lamb)

Serves: 4-5

Ingredients:

- 2 ¼ pounds leg of lamb, rinsed, thawed if frozen
- 6 cloves garlic, sliced
- 2 sprigs fresh rosemary
- Freshly ground pepper to taste
- ½ teaspoon ground cloves
- 1 tablespoon butter, softened
- 1 teaspoon ground allspice
- Salt to taste
- ½ teaspoon dried thyme

Method:

1. Add thyme, spices, salt and butter into a small bowl and stir. Rub this mixture all over the lamb.
2. Take a sharp knife and make small slits at different spots all over the lamb.
3. Stuff garlic slices and rosemary sprigs in the slits and place on a roasting pan.
4. Bake in a preheated oven at 400° F for about 15 minutes. Lower the temperature of the oven to 350° F or cook for about 30-40 minutes or until cooked through and slight pink in color.
5. Remove the pan from the oven and cover the lamb with foil. Let it sit for 15 minutes.
6. Slice and serve.

Reuben Casserole

Serves: 4

Ingredients:

- 1 can (10.75 ounces) condensed cream of mushroom soup
- 1 small onion, chopped
- 1 can (16 ounces) sauerkraut, rinsed, squeezed of excess moisture
- ¾ pound kielbasa sausage, cut into ½ inch pieces
- 6 tablespoons whole wheat bread crumbs
- ¾ cup milk
- ½ tablespoon prepared mustard
- 4 ounces dry egg noodles
- 1 cup Swiss cheese, shredded
- 1 tablespoon butter, melted

Method:

1. Whisk together in a bowl, milk, soup, mustard and onion.
2. Grease a baking dish with a little cooking spray.
3. Add sauerkraut into the dish and spread it evenly.
4. Place the noodles over the sauerkraut. Pour the soup mixture over the noodles.
5. Spread sausage over the noodles followed by cheese.
6. Mix together in a bowl, breadcrumbs and butter and sprinkle over the cheese.
7. Cover the dish with foil tightly.
8. Bake in a preheated oven at 350° F for about 40-60 minutes or until the noodles are cooked.

Breaded Pork Tenderloin

Serves: 8

Ingredients:

- 2 pounds pork tenderloin, cut crosswise into ½ inch slices
- 2/3 cup cornbread/muffin mix
- Pepper to taste
- 2 large eggs, beaten
- 2/3 cup all-purpose flour
- ½ cup canola oil, divided
- 1 teaspoon salt
- Ranch or barbecue sauce to serve (optional)

Method:

1. Add muffin mix, flour, pepper and salt into a bowl and stir.
2. First dip the pork slices in the bow of eggs. Shake to drop off excess egg. Next dredge in flour mixture.
3. Pat on the pork pieces so that the flour sticks to the pork. Place on a plate.
4. Place a large skillet over medium heat. Add a little oil. When the oil is heated, place a few pieces of pork. Cook for 3-4 minutes. Flip sides and cook the other side for 3-4 minutes or until cooked through.
5. Remove with a slotted spoon and place on a plate lined with paper towels.
6. Cook the remaining in batches, follow steps 4-5.
7. Serve with sauce if using.

Polish Pork / Ham Hocks with Beer-Honey Glaze (Golonka)

Serves: 2

Ingredients:

For the hocks:

- 2 large pork hocks or ham hocks, fresh or smoked
- 1 bay leaf
- 1 juniper berry (optional)
- 1 medium onion, peeled, quartered
- 1 small rib celery
- ½ tablespoon fresh parsley, chopped
- ½ tablespoon salt, use lesser if using smoked hocks
- 3 whole black peppercorns
- 1 medium carrot, peeled
- 1 small piece parsnip
- 1 clove garlic, minced
- ½ teaspoon caraway seeds (optional)

For glaze:

- ¼ can beer
- 1 tablespoon cooked liquid
- 1-2 tablespoons honey

Method:

1. Get rid of any hair on the hocks by moving it over flame (hold with tongs). Rinse and place in a Dutch oven or soup pot.
2. Pour enough water to cover the hocks. Water should be at least 3-4 inches above the hocks.

3. As it begins to boil, you will notice that scum will be formed on the top of the water. Discard scum that is floating.
4. Add rest of the ingredients and stir. Lower the heat and cook for a couple of hours or until the meat will start coming off the bones. Turn off the heat.
5. Remove the hocks with tongs and place in a baking dish. Use a tablespoon of the cooked liquid. The rest of the stock can be used in some other recipes.
6. To make glaze: Add all the ingredients for glaze into a small saucepan. Place the saucepan over medium heat. Stir until honey dissolves completely.
7. Pour the glaze over the hocks in the baking dish.
8. Bake in a preheated oven at 375° F for about 30-40 minutes. Baste with the glaze a couple of times while it is baking.

Kielbasa Hot Potato Slaw

Serves: 8

Ingredients:

For sauce mixture:

- 3 teaspoons cornstarch
- 2 tablespoons honey
- ½ teaspoon pepper or to taste
- 2 tablespoons canola oil
- ½ cup cider vinegar
- 2 teaspoons Dijon mustard

For potato slaw:

- 4 medium red potatoes (16 ounces) cut into ½ inch cubes
- 1 cup sweet red pepper, chopped
- 2 packages (14 ounces each) smoked turkey kielbasa, cut into ¼ inch slices
- 1 cup onion, sliced
- 8 strips bacon, cooked, crumbled
- 2 packages (14 ounce each) coleslaw mix
- 2 teaspoons beef bouillon granules
- 1 cup water
- ½ teaspoon salt or to taste

Method:

1. Place a large skillet over medium high heat. Add oil. When the oil is heated, add sausage, onion, potatoes, bacon and red pepper and cook until sausage is brown.

2. Stir in the water and bouillon granules. When it begins to boil, lower the heat and cover with a lid. Simmer until the potatoes are nearly cooked.
3. Stir in the coleslaw and cover again. Cook until tender.
4. Mix together all the sauce ingredients into a bowl and pour into the pan. Stir constantly until the mixture thickens.
5. Cook for 3-5 minutes.
6. Serve hot.

Polish Chicken and Dumplings

Serves: 4

Ingredients:

For the chicken:

- 1 ½ pounds chicken
- 1 small stalk celery with its leaves
- 1 small onion, chopped
- ½ teaspoon ground allspice
- Salt to taste
- ½ teaspoon seasoning salt
- ½ teaspoon dried basil
- ½ tablespoon poultry seasoning
- ½ teaspoon pepper or to taste
- 5 ½ ounces condensed cream of chicken soup (optional)

For dumplings:

- 1 tablespoon olive oil
- 2 cups all-purpose flour
- ½ teaspoon pepper
- ½ tablespoon salt
- 2 eggs
- 1 cup water

Method:

1. To make chicken: Add all the ingredients for chicken except cream of chicken soup into a pot. Pour water to fill the pot. Place the pot over high heat. When it begins to boil, lower the heat and cook for a couple of hours until the chicken is cooked through.

2. Strain the broth into a bowl. Remove the chicken from the strainer and set aside. Discard the other solids.
3. Pour the broth back into the pot. Place it back over medium heat. Add cream of chicken soup.
4. To make dumplings: Add eggs, salt, pepper, o, l and water into a mixing bowl. Mix until well combined.
5. Add flour and mix until well combined and free from lumps.
6. Drop spoonfuls of the mixture into the simmering broth. Stir.
7. Cover with a lid and cook for about 15 minutes.
8. When the chicken is cool enough to handle, discard the bones from the chicken and cut into pieces. Add it into the pot. Heat thoroughly and serve.

Chapter Five: Polish Dessert Recipes

Placek z Sliwkami (Polish Plum Cake)

Serves: 20-24

Ingredients:

For dry ingredients:

- 4 2/3 cups all-purpose flour
- 1 ½ teaspoon salt
- 5 teaspoons baking powder
- 1 ½ cups sugar

For wet ingredients:

- 1 cup butter, at room temperature
- 4 large eggs, at room temperature
- 1 ½ cups milk

For the plum layer:

- 80 fresh plums, any variety, pitted, halved
- ½ teaspoon ground cloves
- ½ cup sugar
- 6 tablespoons butter, chilled, cut into small cubes

Method:

1. Add all the dry ingredients into a large bowl and stir.
2. Add the wet ingredients into the bowl of dry ingredients and beat with an electric mixer set on medium speed for 3-4 minutes or until well-combined and free from lumps.

3. Grease a large baking dish with cooking spray. You can also use 2 smaller baking dishes if desired. Line with parchment paper.
4. Spoon the batter into the baking dish.
5. For the plum layer: Place the plum on the batter, with the cut side facing up. Press the plum slightly so that it is slightly embedded in the batter.
6. Place sugar and cloves in a bowl and stir. Add butter and cut the butter into the mixture until crumbly in texture.
7. Scatter this mixture over the plums.
8. Place rack in the center of the oven.
9. Bake in a preheated oven at 350° F for about 40 -50 minutes or until a toothpick when inserted in the cake at different spots should come out clean. Do not open the oven door for 40-50 minutes.
10. Let the cake rest in the pan until it cools completely. This is done so that the cake absorbs the juices released by the plums and the cake turns out moist.
11. Slice and serve.

Polish Apple Cake

Serves: 24

Ingredients:

For dry ingredients:

- 4 2/3 cups all-purpose flour
- 1 ½ teaspoon salt
- 5 teaspoons baking powder
- 1 ½ cups sugar

For wet ingredients:

- 1 cup butter, at room temperature
- 4 large eggs, at room temperature
- 1 ½ cups milk

For the apple layer:

- 8 large apples, cored, peeled, thinly sliced
- ½ teaspoon ground cloves
- ½ cup sugar
- 6 tablespoons butter, chilled, cut into small cubes

Method:

1. Add all the dry ingredients into a large bowl and stir.
2. Add the wet ingredients into the bowl of dry ingredients and beat with an electric mixer set on medium speed for 3-4 minutes or until well-combined and free from lumps.
3. Grease a large baking dish with cooking spray. You can also use 2 smaller baking dishes if desired. Line with parchment paper.
4. Spoon half the batter into the baking dish.

5. For the apple layer: Place half the apple slices on the batter. Retain about a cup of batter and spoon the remaining batter over the apple slices evenly. The apples should be covered with the batter.
6. Place the remaining apple slices over the batter. Spoon the retained batter at different spots on the apples.
7. Place sugar and cloves in a bowl and stir. Add butter and cut the butter into the mixture until crumbly in texture.
8. Scatter this mixture over the batter.
9. Place rack in the center of the oven.
10. Bake in a preheated oven at 350° F for about 40 -50 minutes or until a toothpick when inserted in the cake at different spots should come out clean. Do not open the oven door for 40-50 minutes.
11. Let the cake rest in the pan until it cools completely. This is done so that the cake absorbs the juices released by the apples and turns moist.
12. Slice and serve.

Sernik (Cheesecake)

Serves: 8-10

Ingredients:

For crust:

- 1 cup all-purpose flour
- ½ teaspoon baking powder
- 1 large egg yolk
- ¼ cup sugar
- 2 ½ ounces cold butter
- 1 ½ tablespoons sour cream

For filling: All the ingredients should be at room temperature

- 2 ½ ounces butter
- 3 large eggs, separated
- ½ tablespoon Kirsch (optional)
- ½ tablespoon flour
- ½ cup sugar
- ½ teaspoon vanilla extract
- 6 tablespoons dried cranberries
- 1 pound traditional Polish cheese twarog

Method:

1. Place the traditional Polish cheese twarog in a strainer for a couple of hours. Transfer into a blender and blend until smooth.
2. Beat the whites until stiff peaks are formed.
3. To make crust: Add flour, baking powder and sugar into a mixing bowl.

4. Add butter and cut it into the mixture until crumbs are formed.
5. Whisk together yolk and sour cream and add into the mixing bowl. Stir until just combined. If the mixture is too hard, sprinkle some water or add an egg.
6. Grease a small baking pan.
7. Place the dough on your countertop and roll with a rolling pin until it is big enough to fit the bottom of the pan and the sides as well.
8. Carefully lift the dough and place in the pan. Press the rolled dough to fit the pan.
9. Crimp the edges of the dough.
10. To make filling: Add butter and sugar into a mixing bowl and beat with an electric mixer set on medium speed until creamy and light.
11. Beat in the yolks, kirsch and vanilla and beat until well combined.
12. Add cranberries and flour into the food processor bowl and pulse until finely chopped and well combined.
13. Transfer into the mixing bowl. Add twarog and stir.
14. Add about ½ cup of the beaten whites into the filling and stir.
15. Add remaining whites and fold gently.
16. Spoon the filling on the prepared crust.
17. Bake in a preheated oven at 350° F for about 40 -50 minutes or until the center jiggles slightly.
18. Let it cool completely at room temperature. Chill for a few hours.
19. Slice and serve.

Budyn (Vanilla pudding)

Serves: 6

Ingredients:

- 4 cups milk
- 6 tablespoons vanilla sugar
- 4 tablespoons potato starch
- 2 tablespoons butter
- 1 vanilla pod, scrape the seeds
- 4 egg yolks

Method:

1. Add 3 cups milk, sugar, butter and vanilla seeds into a heavy bottom saucepan.
2. Place the saucepan over medium heat. Allow it to boil.
3. Whisk together 1-cup milk, potato starch and yolks into a bowl and pour into the saucepan, when the milk begins to boil.
4. Reduce the heat to low heat. Stir constantly until the mixture is thick. Turn off the heat. Do not boil. If by chance you discover some lumps in the mixture, transfer into a blender and blend until smooth.
5. Divide equally into 6 dessert bowls. Cool for a while.
6. Serve warm or chill and serve later.

Ciasteczka Waniliowe (Vanilla Cookies)

Makes: 30 cookies

Ingredients:

- 3 ½ ounces butter, softened
- ½ vanilla bean, scrape the seeds
- 1 cup all-purpose flour
- 2-3 teaspoons milk
- ½ tablespoon confectioners' vanilla sugar
- ¼ cup sugar
- 1 3/4 ounces almonds, ground
- ¼ teaspoon baking powder
- ½ tablespoon confectioners' sugar

Method:

1. Add butter and ¼ cup sugar into a mixing bowl. Beat with an electric mixer until creamy.
2. Add vanilla bean seeds and almonds and beat again.
3. Add flour and baking powder into a bowl and stir.
4. Add the flour mixture into the mixing bowl and mix until well combined into smooth dough. Add milk if the dough is crumbling or very dry.
5. Make 30 equal portions of the dough and shape into half-moons.
6. Place on a baking sheet lined with parchment paper.
7. Bake in a preheated oven at 350° F for about 5-10 minutes or until the underside is golden brown.
8. Remove the baking sheet from the oven.
9. Mix together confectioner's sugar and vanilla confectioners' sugar in a bowl and sprinkle over the hot cookies.

10. Transfer into an airtight container when the cookies are cooled completely.

Paczki (Donuts)

Serves: 6

Ingredients:

- ½ package instant yeast
- 1 large egg yolk
- 1 tablespoon melted butter
- 1 ¾ cups all-purpose flour
- A pinch salt
- ½ cup whole milk
- 2 tablespoons white sugar
- ¼ teaspoon vanilla
- Oil for frying, as required
- Jam of your choice or custard, for filling the donuts
- Granulated sugar to dredge

Method:

1. Pour milk into a saucepan. Place the saucepan over medium heat. When tiny bubbles begin to form around the edges, turn off the heat and allow it to cool until it is lukewarm.
2. Add yeast into the milk and let it sit for 5 minutes.
3. Stir in ½ cup flour and mix until well combined. Set aside for 30 minutes until frothy.
4. Add yolk into a bowl and whisk until it is pale in color.
5. Add butter into the bowl of yeast mixture. Stir in the sugar and mix until well combined.
6. Stir in salt, vanilla and yolk. Add remaining flour, a little at a time and mix well each time. When all the flour has been added, you should be left with moist and soft dough. The dough should not be sticky.

7. Place the dough in a large greased bowl. Cover with plastic wrap. Place in a warm place for a couple of hours or until it doubles in size.
8. Dust your countertop with a little flour. Place the risen dough on it. Punch the dough for a couple of minutes.
9. Roll the dough into a circle of about ½ inch thickness.
10. Carve out the donuts with a 3-inch cookie cutter. Place the donuts on a baking sheet lined with parchment paper. Cover the baking sheet and set aside for 30-40 minutes or until it doubles in size.
11. Place a small deep pan over medium heat. Pour enough oil to cover about 2 inches from the bottom of the pan.
12. When the oil is well heated but not smoking (temperature of oil should be 360° F), add 1-2 donuts. Fry until golden brown. Flip sides and cook the other side until darkish golden brown. Fry only 1-2 at a time. Fry the remaining in batches.
13. Remove the donuts with a slotted spoon and place on a wire rack for 30 seconds.
14. Dredge the donuts in sugar after cooling for 30 seconds. Cool completely.
15. Take a sharp knife and make a slit on the side.
16. Add jam or custard into a piping bag and pipe into the slit.
17. Serve.

Szarlotka (Traditional Polish Apple Tart)

Serves: 4

Ingredients:

For tart dough:

- 6 ½ tablespoons butter, cut into small cubes
- ¾ cup all-purpose flour
- ½ tablespoon heavy cream
- 3 tablespoons powdered sugar
- Yolk of a small egg

For apple filling:

- 1 ½ pounds apples like Granny Smith, cored, cut into ½ inch cubes
- ½ cup sugar or to taste
- ½ teaspoon lemon juice
- ½ teaspoon ground cinnamon (optional)

For glaze:

- 1 tablespoon heavy cream

Method:

1. For tart dough: Add flour and sugar into a mixing bowl.
2. Add butter and cut it into the mixture until crumbs are formed.
3. Whisk together yolk and cream and add into the mixing bowl. Add into the mixing bowl and mix until smooth dough is formed.
4. Wrap the dough in cling wrap and chill for 2 hours.
5. For filling: Add apples and lemon juice into a nonstick pan. Place over medium heat. Cook until nearly dry.

The apples should not be soft. Turn off the heat and cool completely. Add sugar and cinnamon and mix well.

6. Dust your countertop with a little flour. Take out 2/3 of the dough and place on your countertop. With a rolling pin, roll into a circle for about 6-7 inches.

7. Place in a 6-inch tart or pie pan. Press on to the bottom as well as the sides of the pan. Place the dish in the refrigerator for 30 minutes.

8. Bake in a preheated oven at 375° F for about 10-15 minutes or until light golden brown in color. Place some pie weight or something heavy on the piecrust while it is baking. Remove the weights once the pie is baked.

9. Roll the remaining dough into a circle of ¼ inch thickness. Make ½ inch strips using a pizza cutter. Remove the strips and place on a flat plate.

10. Spread the apples over the crust. Place the strips over the filling in a crisscross manner.

11. Brush cream over the strips. Bake for some more time until the apples are bubbling. Remove from the oven and cool.

12. Serve cold or warm or at room temperature.

Babka Wielkanocna (Traditional Easter Babka)

Serves: 24

Ingredients:

For cake:

- 2 ½ teaspoons active dry yeast
- 12 ounces salted butter, chilled
- 1 teaspoon salt
- 2 teaspoons vanilla
- 2 cups + 2 tablespoons all-purpose flour
- 1-2 cups raisins
- ½ cup warm water (less than 110° F)
- 1 ½ cups sugar
- 2 cups scalded milk
- 6 large eggs, at room temperature, beaten
- 4 tablespoons lemon zest, grated (optional)
- Confectioners' sugar, as required

For optional icing:

- 1 1/3 cups confectioners' sugar
- 2 tablespoons boiling water
- 4 tablespoons lemon juice

Method:

1. Add warm water and yeast in a small bowl. In a while the mixture will be frothy.
2. Add butter, sugar and salt into a large mixing bowl. Add milk. Fix the paddle attachment to your mixer. Mix until well combined.
3. Add vanilla and eggs and mix until well combined. Pour the yeast mixture and mix again.

4. Mix in the flour, raisins and lemon zest. The batter will be thick in consistency.
5. Grease 2 babka pans or kugelhopf pans or Turk's head pans) of 10 inches each with cooking spray.
6. Divide the batter equally among the pans. Set aside the pans in a warm place. When it doubles in size or until it reaches the top of the pan, place in a preheated oven.
7. Bake in a preheated oven at 350° F for about 40-45 minutes or if a toothpick is inserted in the center, it should come out clean. Remove the cake from the oven and cool completely. Bake the cakes in batches.
8. For optional icing: Add confectioner's sugar, boiling water and lemon juice into a bowl and whisk until smooth and well combined.
9. Pour over the cake.
10. Cake can be stored in an airtight container, at room temperature for 6-7 days. You can also wrap in cling wrap and place in a freezer safe bag. Freeze for 6 months.

Conclusion

I want to thank you once again for purchasing this book.

If you aren't Polish, then I hope the recipes in this book will introduce you to new methods of cooking, textures, flavor combinations as well as ingredients. Did you ever cook with celery root or leek? Do you want to learn to make delicious pork cutlets that will melt in your mouth? Do you want to learn to make fermented pickles or beets? Well, within the pages of this book, you will have learned about all this and much more.

It is not only a joy to cook traditional Polish recipes, but it will also take you on a food adventure that will change your perspective toward food. You will learn to enjoy cooking food and will also learn to savor the food you cook. It will help you reconnect with real food that will warm your soul.

All the recipes mentioned in this book are simple to understand and easy to follow. You will be able to cook delicious and authentic Polish food within no time, if you follow the recipes given in this book. Make sure that you carefully read and follow the recipes. Also, be careful when you weigh and measure the ingredients. If you want to cook like a pro, then stick to the recipes given. All that you need to do is gather the necessary ingredients, select a recipe that strikes your fancy and start cooking. Perhaps the next time you have guests over for a meal, you can cook them a traditional Polish meal that will blow them away.

Finally, if you enjoyed this book then I'd like to ask you for a favor. Will you be kind enough to leave a review for this book on Amazon? It would be greatly appreciated!